A Guide to Analysis, Design & Implementation Techniques

for the

GCSE Computer Science

Non Exam Assessment

with

Python   or

Python & SQLite

Suitable for all Exam Boards including

CIE pre-release

Worked step by step examples

using previous NEAs

H Sarah Shakibi

October 2017

Contents

Introduction

The Non Exam Assessment for the GCSE (iGCSE) in Computer Science is roughly one of 3 genres:

1. Basic Admin Task
2. Database Task
3. Board Game Task

In this guide we will look at the first two genres and show the **Basic Programming Techniques** required to successfully analyse, design and implement examples of these tasks.

Basic Admin Task

In this type of scenario we typically have a User who will be accessing the computer system through a basic login procedure in order to carry out various administrative tasks.

The system has two main components:

- Front-end (usually Python Shell)
- Back –end (a one-table or 'flat' database using a text file)

Consider the following example from the CIE exam board which shares many features with similar tasks from OCR and EdExcel.

Worked Example – The School Theme Park Trip

In order to take their students on a trip to a Theme Park, a school requires a basic computer system that can:

1. Store the cost of the coach
2. Store the cost of a ticket
3. Store the name and tutor group of each student
4. Store if the student has paid or not
5. Generate a report to show who has not paid
6. Generate an 'expenses' report for each student = (number of students going/350) + 30
7. The total fixed cost for the coach is £350.
8. The fixed cost of an entry ticket is £30.

In order to create a basic computer application for the above requirements, the exam boards usually require pupils to show understanding of the various phases of the basic **Systems Life Cycle:**

- Analysis
- Design
- Implementation
- Testing
- Evaluation

Analysis

teach pupils to extract 'key words' from task to create

Evaluation

How does the implementation match up with the Success

Design

How to translate the Success Criteria into

Testing

Validation, Extreme, Typical & Erroneous

Implementation

How to convert Algorithms into clean Python Code using the Basic Python Toolkit

Analysis & Success Criteria

The requirements for the Analysis Phase are generally the following (this is from OCR but all Boards have approximately the same requirements):

- **Detailed analysis of requirements to solve problem**
- **Clear & logical decomposition of larger tasks into components**
- **Clear Requirements Spec covering ALL of functionality**
- **Approaches are justified (selections, iterations used)**
- **Detailed discussion of testing & success criteria**
- **Importance of validation to produce a robust program**
- **Objectives are clear and show awareness of the need for real-world utility and robustness.**

How do we link these criteria to the requirements stated in the scenario of the problem?

Technique 1 : Extract the key words from the scenario

Read the scenario carefully and highlight the various words which can be linked *directly* to the criteria above:

In order to take their students on a trip to a Theme Park, a school requires a basic computer system that can:

1. Store the cost of the coach
2. Store the cost of a ticket
3. Store the name and tutor group of each student
4. Store if the student has paid or not
5. Generate a report to show who has not paid
6. Generate an 'expenses' report for each student (number of students going/350) + 30
7. The total fixed cost for the coach is £350.
8. The fixed cost of an entry ticket is £30.

Technique 2 : Turn the key words into programming requirements

> - The cost of the coach is a constant and can be hard coded
> - The cost of an entry ticket is a constant and can be hard coded
> - The name of the student needs to be broken into Surname + First Name
> - The First Name & Surname need to be stored in a text file
> - For each student in the text file 'Paid' or 'Not Paid' needs to be added – in this case the data type is Boolean.
> - Generate a report means interrogate the data stored in the text file
> - Interrogate the data means 'run a query'
> - Run a query means select various fields from the text file and add various conditions

Technique 3: Analyse the INPUT,PROCESS, OUTPUT & STORAGE Requirements

Always make sure you refer to the most fundamental diagram in creating an application. Ask yourself what are the INPUTS, PROCESSES, OUTPUTS & STORAGE required?

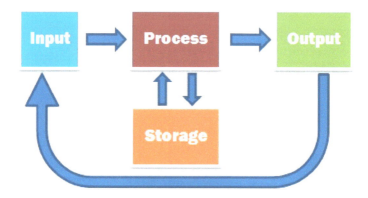

In order to complete the Analysis for the system you are creating you can always create a table for the required components. Look at the example below and note how each Input, Process, Output and Storage needs to be broken down to its **atomic components.**

Remember to include the data type for each input.

State where & how you are going to store the input.

INPUT & Data Type	PROCESS	STORAGE	OUTPUT
Surname - Text	Write to list → write to text file	Text file	
First Name - Text	Write to list → write to text file	Text file	
Paid (Y/N) – Boolean	Write to list → write to text file	Text file	
	Read Text File For each line in which there is 'N' print line to screen		Report showing who has not paid
	Read Text File Count Number of students that have paid Divide 350 by this number Add 30		Expenses Report

Worked Example 2: Login with username & password

The majority of NEA tasks require the user to login with a username and password.

Though the requirements for the creation of a password differ from one Board to the next, the *most basic* login (used in the OCR Sample task 1 of 2016) has the Input, Process, Output & Storage requirements shown below.

These can of course be refined according to further requirements of the Board.

INPUT	PROCESS		OUTPUT
Username	Compare against hard coded user name		
	IF Username correct prompt user for password		Prompt for password
	ELSE ask for Username again (loop)		Prompt for re-entry of Username
Password	Compare against hard coded password		
	IF password correct load Menu		Load Menu Screen
	ELSE ask for password again (loop)		Prompt for re-entry of Password

Technique 4: How to refine the Analysis & create Modular System Functionalities

Based on the analysis of the Inputs, Processes, Outputs and Storage we can draw up this more refined set of **functionalities** for our system in a **modular way**. This needs you to think about the various 'screens' that will appear for the user as they work their way through the choices.

Here is an example from the Theme Park scenario:

- ➤ **An Entry Menu: This will prompt the user to input their Username and Password**
- ➤ **If either the username or password are incorrect then user is prompted to re-enter until they get this right**
- ➤ **If both Username & Password are correct then system should display the main menu**
- ➤ **Option 1: Enter Names of students & if Paid or Not and store details**
- ➤ **Option 2: Generate a report of students who have not paid**
- ➤ **Option 3: Generate an 'Expenses' report**

You are now ready to start the Design phase of the Systems Life Cycle for your application.

Design

The Design phase of any NEA is probably the most difficult because you have to write pseudo-code! However, if you ensure that they have created the **Structured English** version of the pseudocode then this becomes a lot easier (more on this later).

The requirements for this section of the NEA are broadly speaking the following (again OCR is used but other Boards are very similar):

- **All components clearly planned**
- **Discussing & planning of the user interface**
- **Full set of <u>detailed algorithms</u> representing a solution to each part of the problem**
- <u>**Complete enough to be the basis for coding**</u>
- **Detailed discussing of testing & success criteria**
- **Awareness of why testing should be destructive**
- **Variables & data structures identified – use of meaningful names!!**
- **Consideration of how to build in robustness**
- **Clearly designed in a modular way**

Technique 5: Designing the main modules/screens of the system

Using our Theme Park Scenario the main **modules** (and submodules) of the system are:

1. Login or entry menu
2. Main menu
   a) Student Entry (sub-menu)
   b) Generate Report of who has not paid (sub-menu)
   c) Generate Expenses report (sub-menu)

In the Design section of your write-up you need to have **_a drawing_** for each screen of the system:

LOGIN / ENTRY MENU SCREEN DESIGN

MAIN MENU SCREEN DESIGN

Welcome to the Main Menu (**username**)

Please choose one of the options below:

1. **Enter students going on trip**
2. **Generate report of who has not paid**
3. **Generate Expenses report**

Please enter your option:

Sub-menu 1: Enter students going on trip

> How many students would you like to enter [   ]
>
> **Enter surname of student :** [   ]
> **Enter first name of student:** [   ]
> **Enter Tutor Group of student:** [   ]
> **Enter if student has paid or not (Y/N):** [   ]
> **Press any key to exit**

Sub-menu 2: Generate report of who has not paid

> **The following students have not paid:**

Option 3: Generate expenses report

> **Please enter how many students are going on trip:** [   ]
>
> **Based on the number of students going each student needs to pay:**

Technique 6: How to write Structured English Code & pseudocode

Structured English code refers to the writing out of everything which will be eventually coded so we follow these steps:

==Structured English Code → Pseudocode → Code==

This is boring but necessary!

Every pupil wants to just start creating the system by jumping ***directly into code!*** Although this is tempting and faster (usually) it does not always lead to success. Although writing pseudocode is quite tedious it will help you a great deal in finding the possible logical errors before you have begun coding and this does in the long run save on time you would spend debugging your code.

It is recommended that you try the following:

Closed eyes exercise:

In order to work logically through the various menus & modules which are going to be created it is important to be able ==to close your eyes and work through each menu step by step==. You pretend to be using the system and close your eyes to imagine which screen you are in. Then you write down in structured English and in ***logical* order** what steps you have to follow through in each screen of the intended system.

Worked Example 1 : Structured English & Pseudocode for the Login Menu

Structured English Code	Pseudocode
Start System	OUTPUT 'Welcome to the System'
Login Menu is displayed	OUTPUT ' Please login'
User enters username	Username ← USER INPUT
Check username	IF Username = 'Harry'
If incorrect output message to say	Password ← USER INPUT
username was wrong	IF Password = 'password'
Else ask for password	OUTPUT 'Welcome Harry'
User enters password	ELSE OUTPUT 'Please try
If incorrect display message to say	again'
password was wrong	ENDIF
Else welcome user	ELSE OUTPUT 'Please enter
	Username '
	ENDIF

Worked Example 2: Structured English & Pseudocode for the Main Menu

Structured English Code	Pseudocode
Display a looping menu system with options:	OUTPUT 'Welcome to the Main Menu'
	OUTPUT '1. Enter students going on trip'
	OUTPUT '2. Generate report of who has not
1. Enter students going on trip	paid'
2. Generate report of who has not paid	OUTPUT '3. Generate Expenses report'
3. Generate Expenses report	OUTPUT ' Please make your choice'
Please make your choice	Option ← USER INPUT

Worked Example 3: Structured English & Pseudocode for entering & storing student details

Structured English	Pseudocode
OPTION 1 ask how many students to input	OUTPUT 'How many students to input?' Number ← USER INPUT
Ensure the number is an integer – validation (integer – can be extended to see how many exist already)	studentList ← [] FOR i in range Number
	Surname ← INPUT
Create blank list	FirstName ← INPUT
	TutorGroup ← INPUT
FOR the number of students user wishes to enter DO the following:	Paid ← INPUT
	List Append Surname
Prompt user to enter Surname	List Append First name
Prompt user to enter First Name	List Append TutorGroup
Prompt user to enter Tutor Group	List Append Paid
Prompt user to enter Paid (Y/N)	
Append each piece of data to list	
Create strings out of the list elements	
Open text	File Open
append elements from list into f Close text file	File Write
Display main	File Close

Implementation in Python

Technique 7 – Creating a Basic Username & Password Menu

```python
# Basic Username & Login Menu

print('Welcome to....')
print('Please login')

username = None
password = None

while username != 'Somebody':
    username = input('Please enter your username: \t')
while password != 'Something':
    password = input('Please enter your password: \t')

print('Welcome back', username)
```

Output

```
>>> login()
Welcome to....
Please login
Please enter your username:    Somebody
Please enter your password:    Something
Welcome back Somebody
>>>
```

Destructive Testing

```
>>> login()
Welcome to....
Please login
Please enter your username:    harry
Please enter your username:    jones
Please enter your username:    hello
Please enter your username:    Somebody
Please enter your password:    apple
Please enter your password:    box
Please enter your password:    Something
Welcome back Somebody
>>>
```

Technique 8: Creating a Basic Login Menu as a procedure

The only difference here is that we **block indent** the code and add the 'def' line at the top!

```python
# Basic Login Menu as a Procedure


def login():
    print('Welcome to....')
    print('Please login')

    username = None
    password = None

    while username != 'Somebody':
        username = input('Please enter your username: \t')
    while password != 'Something':
        password = input('Please enter your password: \t')

    print('Welcome back', username)
```

Technique 9: Creating a Basic Options Menu

```python
    print('Welcome to ......')
    print()
    print('1. Option 1')
    print('2. Option 2')
    print('3. Option 3')
    print('4. Exit')

    option = int(input('please make your choice'))
```

Destructive Testing Strategy Suggestions:

The variable 'option' is validating the input to integer format.

Normal Data for this input is 1,2,3,4.

Extreme Data is 1,4.

Erroneous Data: Any other character or combination of characters on the keyboard would be wrong and should be rejected.

Presence check: This field should not be left blank.

What should happen if the user inputs a number other than 1-4?

There should be a sensible message output to the user to correct their mistake eg 'Please enter an option number from 1-4'

Technique 10: Creating a Basic Options Menu Procedure

```python
def menu():
    print('Welcome to ......')
    print()
    print('1. Option 1')
    print('2. Option 2')
    print('3. Option 3')
    print('4. Exit')

    option = int(input('please make your choice'))
```

Output

```
>>> menu()
Welcome to ......

1. Option 1
2. Option 2
3. Option 3
4. Exit
please make your choice
```

Technique 11: Creating a looping Menu

```python
def menu():

    loop = True
    while loop:
        print('Welcome to ......')
        print()
        print('1. Option 1')
        print('2. Option 2')
        print('3. Option 3')
        print('4. Exit')

        option = int(input('please make your choice'))

        if option ==4:
            break
```

Technique 12: A menu option to enter and store details (in a list)

```python
def menu1():

    loop = True
    while loop:
        print('Welcome to ......')
        print()
        print('1. Option 1: Enter and store details of persons')
        print('2. Option 2')
        print('3. Option 3')
        print('4. Exit')

        option = int(input('please make your choice'))

        if option ==1:
            number = int(input('How many persons do you want to enter? \t'))

            persons = []              #create blank list

            for i in range(number):    #create a loop to enter all data

                print('Enter surname: ',i+1)
                persons.append(input)
                print('Enter first name: ', i+1)
                persons.append(input)

        if option ==4:
            break
```

Output

```
Welcome to ......

1. Option 1: Enter and store details of persons
2. Option 2 : Search for a person
3. Option 3 : Run a Search Query and show results
4. Option 4: Run a counting Query and show results
5. Exit
please make your choice1
How many persons do you want to enter?  2
Enter surname:  1
Buxton
Enter first name:  1
Jane
Enter surname:  2
Smith
Enter first name:  2
John
['Buxton', 'Jane\n', 'Smith', 'John\n']
Welcome to ......
```

Technique 13: Write contents of a list to a text file for permanent storage

```python
if option ==1:
    number = int(input('How many persons do you want to enter? \t'))

    persons = []            #create blank list

    for i in range(number):    #create a loop to enter all data

        print('Enter surname: ',i+1)
        persons.append(input())
        print('Enter first name: ', i+1)
        persons.append(input()+'\n')

    #create new text file , a+ means append to file not overwrite
    personsfile = open('persons.txt', 'a+')

    #create strings out of the list elements

    personstr = [str(elem) for elem in persons]

    #join up the strings into one line and call it by a variable name 't'
    t=' '.join(personstr)

    #write each line 't' to the text file
    personsfile.write(t)


    #ensure you close the file
    personsfile.close()

    #empty the list ready for re-use
    persons = []
```

If you have a look at the directory in which you have saved your Python file you should also see the text file called 'persons.txt' which has the data entered:

```
persons - Notepad
File  Edit  Format  View  Help

Buxton Jane
 Smith John
```

Technique 14: Search contents of a text file for a given string (eg for a name)

```
if option ==2:

    #create a variable to store the string that user is looking for
    toFind = input('enter the surname you wish to find: \t ')

    #open the text file and read contents line by line
    personsfile = open('persons.txt', 'r')

    #search each line for the string
    for line in personsfile:
        if toFind in line:
            print('Found')
            print(line)

    #don't forget to close the file when you are finished!
    personsfile.close()
```

Output:

```
>>> menu1()
Welcome to ......

1. Option 1: Enter and store details of persons
2. Option 2 : Search for a person
3. Option 3
4. Exit
please make your choice1
How many persons do you want to enter?  1
Enter surname:  1
Roberts
Enter first name:  1
Vicky
Welcome to ......

1. Option 1: Enter and store details of persons
2. Option 2 : Search for a person
3. Option 3
4. Exit
please make your choice2
enter the surname you wish to find:      Roberts
Found
Roberts Vicky
```

Technique 15: Run a Query on a Text File and Output the results

You can run the query for any of the data in the text file.

For example, you can open the persons.txt file *manually* and enter 'M' or 'F' for each person:

```
persons - Notepad
File   Edit   Format   View   Help

shakibi  sarah  F
jones  mark  M

Roberts  Vicky  F
Johnson  Eddie  M
```

Modify the code to ask the user what they are looking for:

```python
if option ==3:

    #if we are looking for all male persons in the file
    toFind = input('What are you looking for?')

    #open the text file and read contents line by line
    personsfile = open('persons.txt', 'r')

    #search each line for the string
    for line in personsfile:
        if toFind in line:
            print(line)

    #don't forget to close the file when you are finished!
    personsfile.close()
```

Now you can run the code again and search for the string 'M' or 'F'

```
>>> menu1()
Welcome to ......

1. Option 1: Enter and store details of persons
2. Option 2 : Search for a person
3. Option 3 : Run a Query and show results
4. Exit
please make your choice3
What are you looking for?M
jones mark M

Johnson Eddie M

Welcome to ......

1. Option 1: Enter and store details of persons
2. Option 2 : Search for a person
3. Option 3 : Run a Query and show results
4. Exit
please make your choice3
What are you looking for?F
shakibi sarah F

Roberts Vicky F
```

Technique 16: Run a Query which counts the number of times a certain piece of data appears in a text file

Manually enter some more data into your 'persons.txt' file (you can do it via Python if you wish to have a challenge)

```
persons - Notepad
File   Edit   Format   View   Help

Shakibi Sarah F
Jones Mark M
Roberts Vicky F
Johnson Eddie M
Michaels Sarah F
Stanton Joe M
Wignall Brendan M
Clifford Lizzie F
```

Suppose we want to count how many male persons we have in our 'persons.txt' file?

Create an extra menu option for this Query:

```python
def menu1():

    loop = True
    while loop:
        print('Welcome to ......')
        print()
        print('1. Option 1: Enter and store details of persons \t')
        print('2. Option 2 : Search for a person \t')
        print('3. Option 3 : Run a Search Query and show results')
        print('4. Option 4: Run a counting Query and show results')
        print('5. Exit')
```

Now create the code for Option 4:

I've made it as general as possible, so you can set the 'toFind' variable to anything that is present in the text file.

There are three cases:

1. One piece of data is found
2. More than one piece of data is found
3. No pieces of matching data are found

```
elif option == 4:

        #first create a counting variable and set it to 0
        count = 0
        #now create a variable for what we are trying to count
        toFind = input('What are you looking for?')
        #open the text file and read contents line by line
        personsfile = open('persons.txt', 'r')
        #search each line for the string and increment the count variable by one each
time
        for line in personsfile:
            if toFind in line:
                count = count + 1
        #output the results to the user
        print('Here are the results:')

        if count ==1:
            print('There is', count, toFind, 'in the file')      #case 1
        elif count >1:
            print('There are', count, toFind, 'in the file')   #case 2
        else:
            print('Sorry, no such data found in the file')    #case 3


        #don't forget to close the file when you are finished!
        personsfile.close()
```

OUTPUT 1: Search for number of males in file

1. Search for 'M'

```
Welcome to ......

1. Option 1: Enter and store details of persons
2. Option 2 : Search for a person
3. Option 3 : Run a Search Query and show results
4. Option 4: Run a counting Query and show results
5. Exit
please make your choice4
What are you looking for?M
Here are the results:
There are 5 M in the file
```

OUTPUT 2: Search for number of females in file

2. Search for 'F'

```
Welcome to ......

1. Option 1: Enter and store details of persons
2. Option 2 : Search for a person
3. Option 3 : Run a Search Query and show results
4. Option 4: Run a counting Query and show results
5. Exit
please make your choice4
What are you looking for?F
Here are the results:
There are 4 F in the file
```

OUTPUT 3: Search number of times a name appears

```
Welcome to ......

1. Option 1: Enter and store details of persons
2. Option 2 : Search for a person
3. Option 3 : Run a Search Query and show results
4. Option 4: Run a counting Query and show results
5. Exit
please make your choice4
What are you looking for?Shakibi
Here are the results:
There is 1 Shakibi in the file
```

OUTPUT 4: When there is 0 count in the file

```
>>> menu1()
Welcome to ......

1. Option 1: Enter and store details of persons
2. Option 2 : Search for a person
3. Option 3 : Run a Search Query and show results
4. Option 4: Run a counting Query and show results
5. Exit
please make your choice4
What are you looking for?sebastian
Here are the results:
Sorry, no such data found in the file
```

SQLite & Python Method

In this section we look at a very powerful tool , SQLite, which uses the robustness of SQL within a Python created basic Graphical User Interface.

The Analysis will exactly be as carried out before however, the Design will now be considerably different.

SQLite 3 is a library in Python which we can use for administrative or database type NEAs.

So far we have relied entirely on lists and text files, so:

What are the advantages of using SQLite?

- ➢ No need to store data temporarily in lists
- ➢ No need to write the contents of the list to a text file
- ➢ Creating Queries becomes much easier

The starting point for using SQLite is to download a very crucial and extremely user-friendly piece of software called DB Browser. Without DB Browser we would not be able to see what is going into our database tables.

Download this from: http://sqlitebrowser.org/

Once downloaded you can open it up using the icon on your desktop. Click it to open this window:

Technique 17: Creating a one table Database with primary key

Run the next piece of code once only! We keep this in a separate table because otherwise if we put it with

the rest of the code we would need a lot more code to ensure that we keep rather than 'drop' the table

each time the code is run – that is a lot of extra work and much more advanced coding (for A Level)

```
import sqlite3

def create_table(db_name,sql):
    with sqlite3.connect(db_name) as db:
        cursor = db.cursor()
        cursor.execute(sql)
        db.commit()

if __name__ =="__main__":
    db_name = "Persons.db"
    sql = """create table Tutees
            (personID integer,
            Surname text,
            Forename text,
            DateOfBirth date,
            HomeAddress text,
            HomeNumber text,
            gender text,
            email text,
            primary key(personID))"""
    create_table(db_name, sql)
```

Now if you now look in the directory in which this Python file was run you will see the following Database has appeared but you can only open this using the DB Browser.

| Persons | 12/06/2017 11:34 | Data Base File | 8 KB |

Open the Persons database and you will see the following:

Name	Type	Schema
∨ ☐ Tables (1)		
> ☐ Person		CREATE TABLE Person (
☐ Indices (0)		
☐ Views (0)		
☐ Triggers (0)		

The Schema for the back-end database

The Schema is the 'blueprint' for the creation of the table and shows **<u>exactly</u>** what you typed into the Python file.

Notice the **DATA DEFINITION** words **CREATE TABLE** followed by the open brackets after which come the name of the various fields together with their *data types*.

This one line contains all the data about the data for the Person table and is sometimes referred to as 'meta-data'.

Schema

CREATE TABLE Person (personID integer, Surname text, Forename text, DateOfBirth date, HomeAddress text, HomeNumber text, gender text, email text, primary key(personID))

Technique 18: Populating the table directly from the database

With the Database open, click on 'Browse Data':

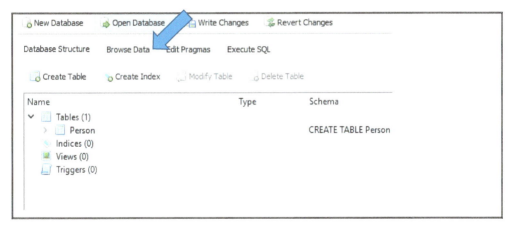

Now click on :

New Record

You will see that the Primary Key field called 'personID' has already been automatically incremented. You can fill in the rest manually if you need to put in a large volume of records:

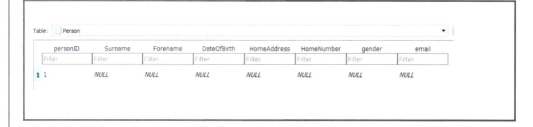

Now add some records manually:

personID	Surname	Forename	DateOfBirth	HomeAddress	HomeNumber	gender	email
Filter	Filter	Filter	Filter	Filter	Filter	Filter	Filter
1 2	bragg	trevor	18/08/1970	london	7777777777	M	blah
2 1	shakibi	sarah	29/09/1958	shropshire	8888888888	F	blah

Technique 19: Populating the table from the GUI using Python

We start from the same basic Options Menu as **before:**

```
def DisplayMenu():
    print()
    print("MAIN MENU")
    print("1. Enter and store person details")
    print("2. Retrieve details of a person")
    print("3. Run Query & Report to Show all persons in database")
    print("4. Run Query & Report to show all females in database")
    print("7. Exit")
```

To add data to our table using Python we need to select **Option 1.**

If the user wishes to add 'n' persons to the table called 'Person' we create a temporary list and from there we push the data into the Person table of the Persons Database:

```
while loop:

  DisplayMenu()

  option = int(input('Please make your choice'))

  if option == 1:

    # ALL OF STEPS 1-6 ARE INSIDE THE 'if option ==1:' STATEMENT!

    #STEP 1

    #create a blank list to take data about persons

    persons = []

    #STEP 2

    #ask user how many persons they wish to enter - ensure it's an integer!

    n = int(input('How many persons do you wish to add?'))

    #STEP 3

    #start loop to ask for data as many times as required

    #STEPS 4,5 & 6 all happen INSIDE the for loop!

    for count in range(0, n):

      personID = int(input('PesonID: '))

      Surname = input('Surname: ')

      Forename = input('Forename: ')

      DateOfBirth = input('Date Of Birth dd/mm/yyyy: ')

      HomeAddress = input('Home Address:  ')

      HomeNumber = input('Home Number:  ')

      gender = input('Gender M/F :')

      email = input('Email: ')


      #STEP 4

      #append the data to the blank list created above

      student.append(personID)

      student.append(Surname)

      student.append(Forename)

      student.append(DateOfBirth)

      student.append(HomeAddress)

      student.append(HomeNumber)

      student.append(gender)

      student.append(Email)
```

```
#STEP 5
#append the data to the blank list created above
persons.append(personID)
persons.append(Surname)
persons.append(Forename)
persons.append(DateOfBirth)
persons.append(HomeAddress)
persons.append(HomeNumber)
persons.append(gender)
persons.append(email)


#STEP 6
#OPEN Database and put data inside table

with sqlite3.connect('Persons.db') as db:
  cursor = db.cursor()
  #use SQL command INSERT and as many '?' marks as pieces of data per person
  #we asked the user to give us 8 pieces of data per person so we need 8 '?' marks
  cursor.execute('INSERT INTO Person VALUES (?,?,?,?,?,?,?,?)', persons)
  db.commit()
```

Here is an example of running the code and adding **one person** to the database:

```
MAIN MENU
1. Enter and store person details
2. Retrieve details of a person
3. Run Query & Report to Show all persons in database
4. Run Query & Report to show all females in database
7. Exit
Please make your choice1
How many persons do you wish to add?1
PersonID:   3
Surname:   jones
Forename:   mark
Date Of Birth dd/mm/yyyy:   blah
Home Address:    blah
Home Number:    blah
Gender M/F :M
Email:  blah
```

Now make sure you check the back-end using the DB Browser to ensure that the data has in fact been added!

personID	Surname	Forename	DateOfBirth	HomeAddress	HomeNumber	gender	email
Filter	Filter	Filter	Filter	Filter	Filter	Filter	Filter
1 1	shakibi	sarah	29/09/1958	shropshire	8888888888	F	blah
2 2	bragg	trevor	18/08/1970	london	7777777777	M	blah
3 3	jones	mark	blah	blah	blah	M	blah

Technique 20: Search for a person with given ID using SQLite

Starting from our Options Menu again:

```
MAIN MENU
1. Enter and store person details
2. Retrieve details of a person
3. Run Query & Report to Show all persons in database
4. Run Query & Report to show all females in database
7. Exit
Please make your choice
```

Select Option 2 and enter the ID of the person only:

```
1. Enter and store person details
2. Retrieve details of a person
3. Run Query & Report to Show all persons in database
4. Run Query & Report to show all females in database
7. Exit
Please make your choice2
Please enter the ID for the person:  1
(1, 'shakibi', 'sarah', '29/09/1958', 'shropshire', '8888888888', 'F', 'blah')
```

Notice that because the PersonID is a *unique identifier* entering a non-existent number would simply have no effect.

We choose **Option 2: Retrieve details of a person**

```
elif choice ==2:   #choice 2 in menu is searching for a person

    #Connect to database

    with sqlite3.connect('Persons.db') as db:

      cursor = db.cursor()

      #ask user for the Person ID number

      id = int(input('Please enter the ID for the person:  '))

      for row in cursor.execute('SELECT * FROM Person WHERE personID=?',(id,)):

        #check to see whether the person is in database or not by

        #temporarily emptying the data into a variable called data

        data = cursor.fetchall()

        if len(data) ==0:

          print('There is no such person in the database')

        else:

          print('Here is the person you are looking for:')

          print(row)
```

Destructive Testing Strategy:

❖ What should happen if the 'id' entered by the user is incorrect?

❖ What should happen if the user does not put in an integer id number?

Technique 21: Produce a report showing every person in the database

```
elif choice ==3:
    with sqlite3.connect("Persons.db") as db:
        cursor = db.cursor()
        cursor.execute('SELECT * from Person ')
        data = cursor.fetchall()
        print(data)
```

Output

```
MAIN MENU
1. Enter and store person details
2. Retrieve details of a person
3. Run Query & Report to Show all persons in database
4. Run Query & Report to show all females in database
7. Exit
Please make your choice3
[(1, 'shakibi', 'sarah', '29/09/1958', 'shropshire', '8888888888', 'F', 'blah'),
 (2, 'bragg', 'trevor', '18/08/1970', 'london', '7777777777', 'M', 'blah'), (3,
 'jones', 'mark', 'blah', 'blah', 'blah', 'M', 'blah')]
```

Technique 22: Produce a report showing only females/males in the database

Here the SQL selection statement WHERE needs a variable (gender) which is **explicitly** set to say 'F' or 'M'

```
elif choice ==4:
    with sqlite3.connect("Persons.db") as db:
        cursor = db.cursor()
        gender = 'F'
        cursor.execute('SELECT * from Person WHERE gender=?',(gender,))
        data = cursor.fetchall()
        print(data)
```

```
MAIN MENU
1. Enter and store person details
2. Retrieve details of a person
3. Run Query & Report to Show all persons in database
4. Run Query & Report to show all females in database
7. Exit
Please make your choice4
[(1, 'shakibi', 'sarah', '29/09/1958', 'shropshire', '8888888888', 'F', 'blah')]
```

Extension suggestion:
Instead of hard coding the gender to 'F' or 'M', you can create user input and validate it.

Worked Example: The Big Movie Database

Scenario

In this task we are required to hold much more information in the database. Crudely speaking, it would still be possible to have a 'flat' database and the GCSE specifications which deal with flat databases are CIE and OCR. This is a good practice task for learning the techniques in Year 10 of the GCSE.

I'll go through the 'flat' database method first using text files and lists. But either way, here are the system requirements:

- **Login Screen where customers either sign-in or join the Movie Club**
- **Customers are given a choice of genres to pick from**
- **In each genre customers are able to see 20 movies**
- **Customers are allowed to have 5 movies at any time**
- **System stores the following data about customers:**
    - **Surname**
    - **First Name**
    - **Username**
    - **Password**
    - **Up to 3 personal preferences**
- **The system stores the following data about movies:**
    - **Genre of movie**
    - **Title**
- **The system should also be able to store which movies a given client has chosen**
- **The system should be able to generate reports based on:**
    - **Customer choices**
    - **Genres which are most popular - statistics**
    - **Ratings of a movie by customers**
    - **Recommendations for future viewings**

Method 1: List & Text file

Creating the entry Menu

```
def main():

    print('Welcome to the Movie Database')
    print()
    print('1. Sign Up - if you do not have an account')
    print('2. Member Login')
    print('3. User Choice Statistics')
```

Technique 23: Sign Up with Username & Password

(all code to be indented under 'if option ==1:')

```
option = int(input('Please choose an option:\t'))
if option ==1:
    print ()
    Surname = input('Surname: \t')
    Firstname = input('Firstname: \t')
    Username = input('Please create a username:\t')
    while True:

        password = input('Please enter your password with at least one capital letter and starting with @:\t')
        if password.lower()== password or password.upper()==password or password.isalnum()==password:
            print('password needs at least one capital letter and one number ')

        elif password.lower()== password and password.upper()==password or password.isalnum()==password:
            print ('password  needs at least one capital letter and one number')

        else:
```

```
        password.lower()== password and password.upper()==password and password.isalnum()==password

        print ('password is acceptable')

        break


    #create blank list for member details
    member = []
    member.append(username)
    member.append(password)
    print()
    print()
```

Destructive Testing Strategy Suggestions:

❖ Check to see if username exists? You can do this by running a SQL query WHERE username = Username

❖ Check for length of password: length check

❖ Check for blank entry: presence check

Technique 24: Collect & Store User Preference

```
print('Please spend a few moments to tell us')
print('some of your personal preferences')

print('Your favourite place for watching movies?')
print('a.At home \t')
print('b.At work \t')
print('c.Travelling \t')

 #create storage variable and append to list
 pref1=input('Please pick a preference:\t')

member.append('Place: '+pref1)
```

```python
print('Your favourite device for watching movies?:\t'
print()
print('d.mobile \t')
print('e.tablet \t')
print('f.PC \t ')

#create storage variable and append to list
pref2=input('pick your device preference')
member.append('Device: '+pref2)

#create storage variable and append to list
pref3=input('pick your favourite time of day:| \t')
member.append('Time: '+pref3)

print('Finally, your favourite genre of movie?')
print('j.Comedy')
print('k.Scifi')
print('l.Drama')
genre = input('please enter your favourite genre:\t')

#create storage variable and append to list
member.append('Genre: '+genre)

 #create strings out of list elements
 #create text file member.txt
 #write contents of list to text file
 memberstr = [str(elem) for elem in member]
 p=' '.join(memberstr)
 memberfile=open('member.txt','a+')
 memberfile.write(p)
 memberfile.write('\n')
 memberfile.close()

#this completes the sign up of the new user
#now ask user to login to start choosing
print('Please login to start choosing your movies')
print('Thank you')
```

OUTPUT: Signing Up

```
>>> main()
Welcome to the Movie Database

1. Sign Up - if you do not have an account
2. Member Login
3. Counting User Choices & making recommendations
Please choose an option:          1

Please create a username:         bragg
Please enter your password with at least one capital letter and starting with @:
@Joey
password is acceptable
```

OUTPUT Collecting User Preferences

```
Please spend a few moments to tell us some of your member
so we can better recommend future films for you
What is your favourite place for watching movies?
a.At home
b.At work
c.Travelling
Please pick a preference:          a




What is your favourite device for watching movies?:

d.mobile
e.tablet
f.PC
pick your device preferencee


What is your favourite time of the for watching movies?

g.Morning
h.Afternoon
i.Evening
pick your favourite time of day for watching movies:     h
```

```
Finally, what is your favourite genre of movie?
j.Comedy
k.Scifi
l.Drama
please enter your favourite genre:        j
Please login to start choosing your movies, thank you
>>> |
```

Check the member.txt file for entries:

```
member - Notepad
File  Edit  Format  View  Help
bragg @Joey Place: a Device: e Time: h Genre: j
```

Technique 25: Member Login, Choosing & Storing Movies

<mark>ALL CODE TO BE INDENTED UNDER OPTION ==2</mark>

```python
elif option==2:
    # this section can be tightened to check for the
    # username & password in the member file first
    username = input('Username:\t')
    password = input('Password:\t')
    print('Welcome back', username)

    #its very easy to put a numbered list
    #of movies in a text file first
    file = open('movies.txt', 'r')

    #create a blank list for temporary
    #storage of user choices
    viewings = []
```

```python
    #ask user to make 5 choices, you can
    #change this to more than 5 choices
    print(' You can make five choices today')
    for i in range(5):
        #read each line in file and print all to screen
        for line in file:
            print(line)
        choice=int(input('please make a choice: \t'))


        #use the choice number to append data
        #to viewings list
        if choice in range(4):
            viewings.append(password)
            viewings.append(choice)
            viewings.append('Comedy \n')
        elif choice in range(5,8):
            viewings.append(password)
            viewings.append(choice)
            viewings.append('Drama \n')
        else:
            viewings.append(password)
            viewings.append(choice)
            viewings.append('Action \n')



#exit loop and confirm user choices
print('Thank you, you have chosen the following movies')
print(viewings)


#create strings out of the viewings list elements
viewingsstr = [str(elem) for elem in viewings]
t=' '.join(viewingsstr)
#write strings to file
viewingsfile=open('viewings.txt','a+')
viewingsfile.write(t)
viewingsfile.write('\n')
viewingsfile.close()
```

OUTPUT:

```
Username:          shakibi
Password:          @shakibi
Welcome back shakibi
 You can make five choices today
1.Comedy 1

2.Comedy 2

3.Comedy 3

4.Comedy 4

5.Action 1

6.Action 2

7.Action 3

8.Action 4

9.Drama 1

10.Drama 2

11.Drama 3

12.Drama 4
please make a choice:    1
please make a choice:    3
please make a choice:    7
please make a choice:    8
please make a choice:    12
```

Check the text file (viewings.txt) for entries:

```
viewings - Notepad
File  Edit  Format  View  Help

@shakibi 1 Comedy
 @shakibi 3 Comedy
 @shakibi 7 Drama
 @shakibi 8 Action
 @shakibi 12 Action
```

Destructive Testing Strategy suggestions:

❖ Check that username exists in the member file – if not it should be rejected with a message that asks the user to input username again

❖ Check that the correct password for the username is entered –if not it should be rejected with a message that asks the user to input password again

❖ What should happen if the user does not enter the correct number for choice? Currently these are numbers between 1-12. There should be a message asking user to input a number between 1 and 12.

Technique 26: Creating User Choice Statistics

All code indented under 'elif option==3'

```
elif option==3:
    viewingsfile=open('viewings.txt','r')
    #set counter variables to 0
    countComedy=0
    countDrama=0
    countAction=0
    #create variables to search viewings file
    comedy = 'Comedy'
    drama = 'Drama'


    #open viewings file for reading and
    #search each line for Comedy,Drama or Action
    for line in viewingsfile:
        if comedy in line:
            countComedy = countComedy + 1
        elif drama in line:
            countDrama = countDrama + 1
        else:
            countAction = countAction + 1
```

```
#output results to user

print('So far you have watched')
print(countComedy, 'Comedies')
print(countDrama, 'Dramas')
print(countAction, 'Action Movies')


#create viewing percentages

total = countComedy + countDrama + countAction
percentComedy = (countComedy/total)* 100
percentDrama = (countDrama/total)* 100
percentAction = (countAction/total)* 100


#put percentage viewings into an empty list

viewingsTotal.append(str(percentComedy) + '% Comedy')
viewingsTotal.append(str(percentDrama) + '% Drama')
viewingsTotal.append(str(percentAction) + '% Action')


#find top percentage
favourite = max(percentComedy,percentDrama,percentAction)
print('Your viewing statistics so far:')
print(viewingsTotal)
```

OUTPUT:

```
>>> main()
Welcome to the Movie Database

1. Sign Up - if you do not have an account
2. Member Login
3. User Choice Statistics
Please choose an option:          3
So far you have watched
3 Comedies
2 Dramas
5 Action Movies
Your viewing statistics so far:
['30.0% Comedy', '20.0% Drama', '50.0% Action']
>>> |
```

Extension Suggestions:

❖ You can use the 'max' function in Python to find the highest percentage

❖ Use this to recommend future movies to the user

Method 2: SQLite & Python

For this method we are going to get a little help from a fantastic resource available on

http://pythonschool.net/databases/searching-and-sorting-data/

Go to this page you will see a link called 'Movie Database'. Download and save the movies database in your directory.

Technique 27 : Using the DB Browser

Start your DB Browser software and go to 'Open Database':

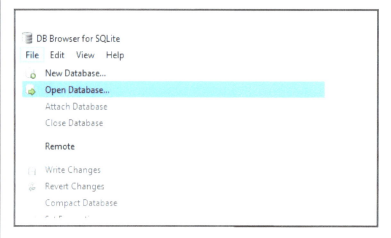

Locate the 'movie' database and click on 'Open':

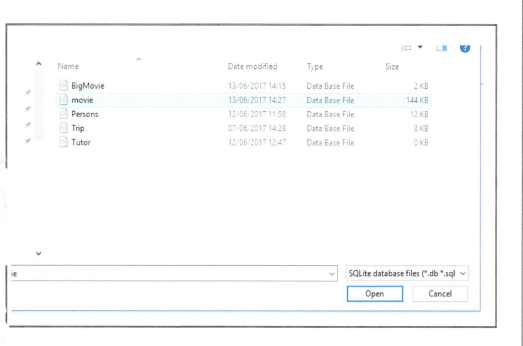

You will see the following tables already present in the database:

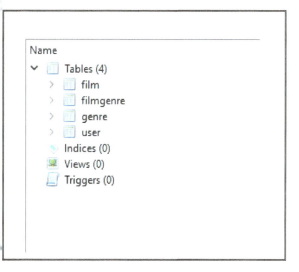

The Schema or blueprint for each table is also shown:

Schema

CREATE TABLE film (filmID integer, title text, releaseYear integer, primary key(filmID))
CREATE TABLE filmgenre (filmgenreID integer, filmID integer, genreID integer, primary key(filmgenreID), foreign key(filmID) references film(filmID))
CREATE TABLE genre (genreID integer, genreName text, primary key(genreID))
CREATE TABLE user (userID integer, userAge integer, userGender text, userOccupation text, userZipCode integer, primary key(userID))

Now click on 'Browse Data':

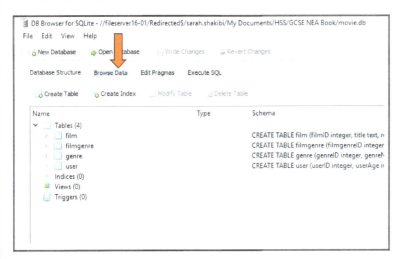

With the 'film' table chosen you can see the following:

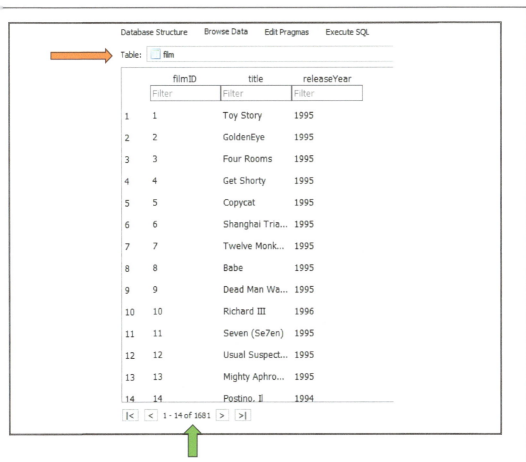

If you look at the bottom you will see **1681 films saved in this table**. This is the reason for choosing to work with this database. Thanks to www.pythonschool.net we don't have to re-invent the wheel and create this database from scratch or spend hours populating it with data.

NB: This is a *relational database* but at GCSE you don't have to worry about the relationships between the various tables.

You do however, need to create two more tables which we need for our purposes.

We will create one of the tables with Python and the other one directly inside the database.

Member Table

```python
import sqlite3

def create_table(db_name, sql):
    with sqlite3.connect(db_name) as db:
        cursor = db.cursor()
        cursor.execute(sql)
        db.commit()

if __name__ =="__main__":
    db_name = "movie.db"
    sql = """create table member
                (MemberID integer,
                Username text,
                password text,
                Surname text,
                Firstname text,
                Interest1 text,
                Interest2 text
                Interest3 text,
                primary key(MemberID))"""
    create_table(db_name, sql)
```

Now check with DB browser that this has been created:

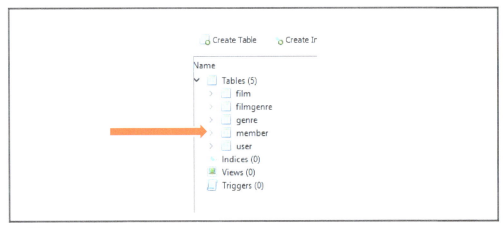

We will populate this table later using Python.

Technique 28 : Creating a table directly in DB Browser

Now we will create the 'viewings' table *directly inside* the DB browser.

First click on 'Create Table':

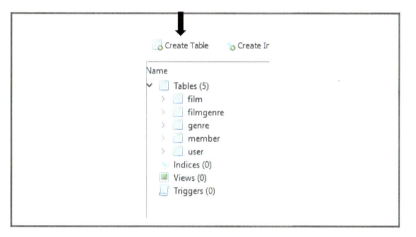

A new dialogue box will open – put the name of the table in the top box:

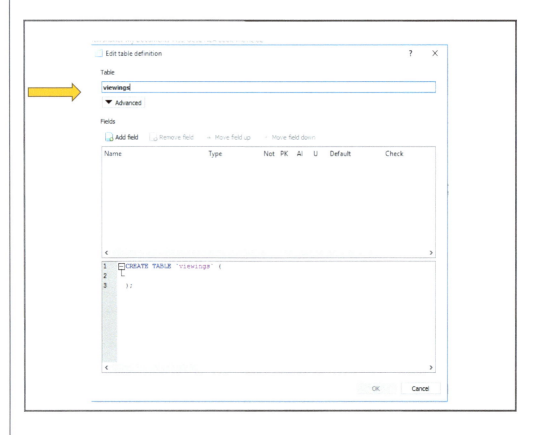

Now click on 'Add Field':

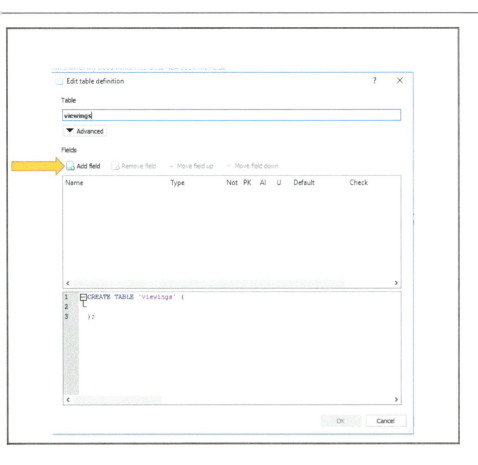

Put in the name of the first field 'viewingID' and make sure you tick the 'PK' and'AI' boxes.

PK = Primary Key – this is the unique identifier for each viewing

AI = Auto Increment – we don't need to remember the last number, it will automatically give the viewing the next number available.

Now create the next 3 fields as shown below (username, choice, genre):

<mark>Make sure you have selected the correct data type for each field!</mark>

<mark>Also be very careful with upper and lower case typing! Username has upper case 'U'!!</mark>

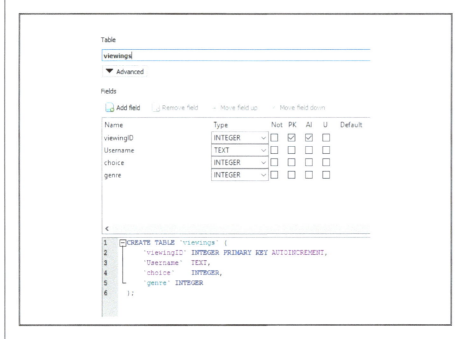

OPTION 1 – Sign Up

The code here is essentially as in Method 1 – but it's given for completeness.

```
File  Edit  Format  Run  Options  Window  Help
    print('3. Exit Database')

    option = int(input('Please choose an option:\t'))

    if option ==1:
        print ()
        Surname = input('Surname: \t')
        Firstname = input('Firstname: \t')
        Username = input('Please create a username:\t')
        while True:

            password = input('Please enter your password with at least one capital letter and starting with @:\t')

            if password.lower()== password or password.upper()==password or password.isalnum()==password:
                print('password needs at least one capital letter and one number ')

            elif password.lower()== password and password.upper()==password or password.isalnum()==password:
                print ('password  needs at least one capital letter and one number')

            else:
                password.lower()== password and password.upper()==password and password.isalnum()==password
                print ('password is acceptable')
                break
```

#We collect the User Interests as before:

```python
print('Please spend a few moments')
print('to tell us some of your interests')
print('----------------------------------------------------')
print('What is your favourite place for watching movies?')
print('a.At home')
print('b.At work')
print('c.Travelling')

Interest1=input('Please pick a preference:\t')

if Interest1 =='a':
    Interest1 = 'At home'
elif Interest1 =='b':
    Interest1 = 'At Work'
else:
    Interest1 = 'Travelling'

print('Your favourite device for watching movies?')
print()
print('d.mobile \t')
print('e.tablet \t')
print('f.PC \t ')


Interest2=input('pick your device preference \t')

if Interest2 =='d':
    Interest2 = 'mobile'
elif Interest2 =='e':
    Interest2 = 'Tablet'
else:
    Interest2 = 'PC'


print('Finally,your favourite genre of movie?')
print('g.Comedy')
print('h.SciFi')
print('i.Drama')
Interest3 = input('your favourite genre:\t')

print('Thank you for your time')
print('Please login to start chocsing')


if Interest3 =='g':
    Interest3 = 'Comedy'
elif Interest3 =='h':
    Interest3 = 'SciFi'
else:
    Interest3 = 'Drama'
```

Technique 29: Creating an INSERT statement in SQLite & Python

Now that collection of data on the user is complete we need the new method of writing to our database (*ensure that this code is indented as above under 'if option ==1'*):

```
with sqlite3.connect('movie.db') as db:

      cursor = db.cursor()

      #create the SQL statement that will INSERT the data into the 'member' table

      sql = 'insert into member (Username, password, Surname, Firstname, Interest1, Interest2, Interest3 ) values
(?,?,?,?,?,?,?)'

      #create the variable that will act as a parameter to insert user input

      values =(Username,password,Surname,Firstname, Interest1, Interest2, Interest3)

      cursor.execute(sql,values)

      db.commit()
```

OUTPUT – SIGN Up

```
>>> main()
Welcome to the Movie Database

1. Sign Up - if you do not have an account
2. Member Login
3. Exit Database
Please choose an option:        1

Surname:        shakibi
Firstname:      sarah
Please create a username:       sarah2
Please enter your password with at least one capital letter and starting with @:
@Hello1
password is acceptable
Please spend a few moments
to tell us some of your interests
----------------------------------------------------
```

```
---------------------------------------------------------------
What is your favourite place for watching movies?
a.At home
b.At work
c.Travelling
Please pick a preference:        a
Your favourite device for watching movies?

d.mobile
e.tablet
f.PC
pick your device preference      f
Finally,your favourite genre of movie?
g.Comedy|
h.Scifi
i.Drama
your favourite genre:    i
Thank you for your time
Please login to start choosing
>>>
```

Check inside DB Browser to see that the data has been entered correctly into the 'member' table:

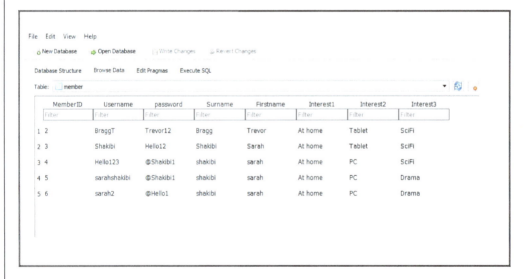

Destructive Testing Strategy Suggestions:

❖ Presence check if username is left blank

❖ Check that username has not been taken before

❖ What should happen if the user does not put '@' at the beginning of their password?

❖ Do a length check on the password

❖ Do a validation on the input of user interests.

❖ Identify what is **Normal, Extreme & Erroneous Data** for Interests 1,2 & 3.

❖ E.g for Interest 1 the Normal Data inputs are **'a', 'b', 'c'**. What should happen if user enters 'g' or any other

letter? Sensible message should guide user to input correct letter.

Technique 30 : Login, Choosing movies & storage with SQLite & Python

OPTION 2 of main menu – login

```python
elif option==2:

        #this section can be tightened to check for username and
        #password in the member file first
        #this is authentication
        Username = input('Username:\t')
        password = input('Password:\t')
        print('Welcome back', Username)

        loop = True
        while loop:

            print('Please choose a genre to see our latest selections')
            print('a.Comedy')
            print('b.SciFi')
            print('c.Drama')
            print('d.Future Recommendations for you')

            choice = input('Please make your choice: \t ')

        if choice == 'a':


        #here we use our first query in SQL to isolate those films with Genre Number = 5 which

        # is comedies

        #filmID is the primary key in the 'film' table and it is imported into 'filmgenre' table as
```

```python
        # a foreign key
    with sqlite3.connect('movie.db') as db:
        cursor = db.cursor()
        cursor.execute('select * from film inner join filmgenre on film.filmID = filmgenre.filmID where
genreID =5 limit 20')
        #we can change limit 20 to limit 30,40 etc to show as many films as required
        #on the screen
        comedies = cursor.fetchall()
        print('Here is a selection of our latest comedies')
        for item in comedies:
            print(item)


        #set up the loop to take user input – 5 films but this can be changed
        for i in range(5):
            choice = int(input('enter your choice'))
            genre = 5
            #create SQL statement to insert the user choices into the 'viewing' table
            sql = 'insert into viewing (Username, choice, genre ) values (?,?,?)'
            # put all input values into a tuple
            values =(Username, choice, genre)
            #enter into table and save
            cursor.execute(sql,values)
            db.commit()
```

```
>>> main()

Welcome to the Movie Database


1. Sign Up - if you do not have an account

2. Member Login

3. Exit Database

Please choose an option:     2

Username:     shakibi

Password:     @Hello1

Welcome back shakibi

Please choose a genre to see our latest selections

a.Comedy

b.SciFi

c.Drama

d.Future Recommendations for you

Please make your choice:     a

Here is a selection of our latest comedies

(1, 'Toy Story', 1995, 3, 1, 5)

(4, 'Get Shorty', 1995, 9, 4, 5)

(8, 'Babe', 1995, 18, 8, 5)

(13, 'Mighty Aphrodite', 1995, 27, 13, 5)

(16, 'French Twist (Gazon maudit)', 1995, 31, 16, 5)

(17, 'From Dusk Till Dawn', 1996, 34, 17, 5)

(21, 'Muppet Treasure Island', 1996, 44, 21, 5)

(25, 'Birdcage, The', 1996, 55, 25, 5)

(26, 'Brothers McMullen, The', 1995, 56, 26, 5)

(29, 'Batman Forever', 1995, 63, 29, 5)

(34, 'Doom Generation, The', 1995, 73, 34, 5)

(40, 'To Wong Foo, Thanks for Everything! Julie Newmar', 1995, 86, 40, 5)

(41, 'Billy Madison', 1995, 87, 41, 5)

(42, 'Clerks', 1994, 88, 42, 5)

(45, 'Eat Drink Man Woman', 1994, 93, 45, 5)
```

(47, 'Ed Wood', 1994, 96, 47, 5)

(49, 'I.Q.', 1994, 99, 49, 5)

(63, 'Santa Clause, The', 1994, 131, 63, 5)

(65, "What's Eating Gilbert Grape", 1993, 133, 65, 5)

(66, 'While You Were Sleeping', 1995, 135, 66, 5)

enter your choice 4

enter your choice 13

enter your choice 29

enter your choice 45

enter your choice 47

Please choose a genre to see our latest selections

Check the 'viewing' table to ensure that the last 5 choices have been entered:

Table: viewing

viewingID	Username	choice	genre
Filter	Filter	Filter	Filter
12 12	shakibi	35	5
13 13	shakibi	36	5
14 14	shakibi	10	5
15 15	shakibi	9	5
16 16	shakibi	4	5
17 17	shakibi	5	5
18 18	shakibi	6	5
19 19	shakibi	10	5
20 20	shakibi	18	5
21 21	shakibi	4	5
22 22	shakibi	13	5
23 23	shakibi	29	5
24 24	shakibi	45	5
25 25	shakibi	47	5

|<   <   12 - 25 of 25   >   >|

The code is repeated exactly for choice of Drama or SciFi

```
elif choice == 'b':   #choice of SciFi  notice that genreID = 15 – rest of code as before


        with sqlite3.connect('movie.db') as db:
          cursor = db.cursor()
          cursor.execute('select * from film inner join filmgenre on film.filmID = filmgenre.filmID where
genreID =15 limit 20')
            scifi = cursor.fetchall()
            print('Here is a selection of our latest SciFi Movies')
            for item in scifi:
              print(item)


            for i in range(5):
              choice = int(input('enter your choice'))
              genre = 15
              sql = 'insert into viewing (Username, choice, genre ) values (?,?,?)'
              values =(Username, choice, genre)
              cursor.execute(sql,values)
            db.commit()
```

TIP: There are 18 different genres in the film database so you can copy this code for as many of the genres as required

Technique 31 : Create a QUERY to show a member's viewings

The most important part of the code is to run the query to show a given User's viewings:

```
elif choice == 'd':   #select films chosen by a given user


        with sqlite3.connect('movie.db') as db:
          cursor = db.cursor()
```

```
                username = input('please re-enter your username')

                #create SQL query to select those choices where a given username is used

                sql = 'select * from viewing inner join film on viewing.choice = film.filmID where Username =
username'

                cursor.execute(sql)

                #fetchall() prints out all the results of the search which we need to assign to

                # a variable – totalviewings in this case

                totalviewings = cursor.fetchall()

                print('Here are your viewings so far')

                print('totalviewings)
```

OUTPUT

>>> main()

Welcome to the Movie Database

1. Sign Up - if you do not have an account

2. Member Login

3. Exit Database

Please choose an option: 2

Username: shakibi

Password: @Hello1

Welcome back shakibi

Please choose a genre to see our latest selections

a.Comedy

b.SciFi

c.Drama

d.Future Recommendations for you

Please make your choice: d

please re-enter your username   shakibi

[(1, 'shakibi', 17, 5, 17, 'From Dusk Till Dawn', 1996), (2, 'shakibi', 21, 5, 21, 'Muppet Treasure Island', 1996), (3,
'shakibi', 26, 5, 26, 'Brothers McMullen, The', 1995), (4, 'shakibi', 65, 5, 65, "What's Eating Gilbert Grape", 1993),
(5, 'shakibi', 66, 5, 66, 'While You Were Sleeping', 1995), (6, 'shakibi', 96, 15, 96, 'Terminator 2: Judgment Day',
1991), (7, 'shakibi', 121, 15, 121, 'Independence Day (ID4)', 1996), (8, 'shakibi', 164, 15, 164, 'Abyss, The', 1989),
(9, 'shakibi', 175, 15, 175, 'Brazil', 1985), (10, 'shakibi', 82, 15, 82, 'Jurassic Park', 1993), (11, 'shakibi', 23, 5, 23,

'Taxi Driver', 1996), (12, 'shakibi', 35, 5, 35, 'Free Willy 2: The Adventure Home', 1995), (13, 'shakibi', 36, 5, 36,

'Mad Love', 1995), (14, 'shakibi', 10, 5, 10, 'Richard III', 1996), (15, 'shakibi', 9, 5, 9, 'Dead Man Walking', 1995),

(16, 'shakibi', 4, 5, 4, 'Get Shorty', 1995), (17, 'shakibi', 5, 5, 5, 'Copycat', 1995), (18, 'shakibi', 6, 5, 6, 'Shanghai

Triad (Yao a yao yao dao waipo qiao)', 1995), (19, 'shakibi', 10, 5, 10, 'Richard III', 1996), (20, 'shakibi', 18, 5, 18,

'White Balloon, The', 1995), (21, 'shakibi', 4, 5, 4, 'Get Shorty', 1995), (22, 'shakibi', 13, 5, 13, 'Mighty Aphrodite',

1995), (23, 'shakibi', 29, 5, 29, 'Batman Forever', 1995), (24, 'shakibi', 45, 5, 45, 'Eat Drink Man Woman', 1994),

(25, 'shakibi', 47, 5, 47, 'Ed Wood', 1994)]

Technique 32 : Rating Movies by a member

If you wish the user to rate the movies they have watched so far then you can use the following technique.

Here we are rating the last ten movies only. We create a new list and slice it to the last ten items.

The starting point is to **Login** and then choose **Option d:**

```
elif option==2:   #the login option

    #this section can be tightened to check for username and
    #password in the member file first
    #this is authentication
    Username = input('Username:\t')
    password = input('Password:\t')
    print('Welcome back', Username)

    loop = True
    while loop:

        print('Please choose a genre to see our latest selections')
        print('a.Comedy')
        print('b.SciFi')
        print('c.Drama')
        print('d.Rating the movies you have watched')

        choice = input('Please make your choice: \t ')

        elif choice == 'd':    #option 'd' - rating the movies


        with sqlite3.connect('movie.db') as db:
            cursor = db.cursor()
            username = input('please re-enter your username')
            sql = 'select * from viewing inner join film on viewing.choice = film.filmID where
```

```
Username = username'  #this should all be typed on one line in Python

                cursor.execute(sql)

                totalviewings = cursor.fetchall()

                print('Here are your viewings so far')

                print(totalviewings)




 #check length of total viewings and choose the last ten entries

 if len(totalviewings) > 10:
     |
     #slice the list to its last ten entries
     totalviewings = totalviewings[-10:]
     print()
     print()
     print('--------------R A T I N G S--------------')
     print()
     print('Here are the last ten movies you have viewed')
     print(totalviewings)
     print()
     print()
     print('Please rate them now - thank you!')
     print('5-Excellent 4-Good 3-Fair 2-Poor 1-Awful')


     #create a variable for the scores of 1-5
     fives = 0
     fours = 0
     threes = 0
     twos = 0
     ones = 0
```

```python
    #create a new blank list for ratings

    ratings =[]

    for item in totalviewings:

        print(item)


        rate = int(input('Please rate this movie?: \t'))

        if rate == 1:
            ones = ones + 1
        elif rate ==2:
            twos = twos + 1
        elif rate ==3:
            threes = threes + 1
        elif rate ==4:
            fours = fours + 1
        elif rate ==5:
            fives = fives + 1
        else:
            print('Not rated')


    #add ratings to the list

    ratings.append(item)
    ratings.append('rating')
    ratings.append(rate)
#produce a print out on screen showing totals
print()
print('-----------THESE ARE YOUR RATINGS----------------')
print(ratings)
print()
print('-----------OUR  RECOMMENDATIONS------------------')
print()
print('Total 5s:', fives)
print('Total 4s:', fours)
print('Total 4s:', threes)
print('Total 4s:', twos)
print('Total 4s:', ones)

#compare totals and recommend future movies

if fives >=5 or fours >=5:
    print('We recommend more comedies')
else:
    print('We recommend another genre for you')
print()
print('Please choose some new movies')
```

OUTPUT

---------------R A T I N G S---------------

Here are the last ten movies you have viewed
[(16, 'shakibi', 4, 5, 4, 'Get Shorty', 1995), (17, 'shakibi', 5, 5, 5, 'Copycat', 1995), (18, 'shakibi', 6, 5, 6, 'Shanghai Triad (Yao a yao yao dao waipo qiao)', 1995), (19, 'shakibi', 10, 5, 10, 'Richard III', 1996), (20, 'shakibi', 18, 5, 18, 'White Balloon, The', 1995), (21, 'shakibi', 4, 5, 4, 'Get Shorty', 1995), (22, 'shakibi', 13, 5, 13, 'Mighty Aphrodite', 1995), (23, 'shakibi', 29, 5, 29, 'Batman Forever', 1995), (24, 'shakibi', 45, 5, 45, 'Eat Drink Man Woman', 1994), (25, 'shakibi', 47, 5, 47, 'Ed Wood', 1994)]

Please rate them now - thank you!
5-Excellent 4-Good 3-Fair 2-Poor 1-Awful
(16, 'shakibi', 4, 5, 4, 'Get Shorty', 1995)
Please rate this movie?:   5
(17, 'shakibi', 5, 5, 5, 'Copycat', 1995)
Please rate this movie?:   5
(18, 'shakibi', 6, 5, 6, 'Shanghai Triad (Yao a yao yao dao waipo qiao)', 1995)
Please rate this movie?:   4
(19, 'shakibi', 10, 5, 10, 'Richard III', 1996)
Please rate this movie?:   5

(20, 'shakibi', 18, 5, 18, 'White Balloon, The', 1995)
Please rate this movie?:   4
(21, 'shakibi', 4, 5, 4, 'Get Shorty', 1995)
Please rate this movie?:   5
(22, 'shakibi', 13, 5, 13, 'Mighty Aphrodite', 1995)
Please rate this movie?:   4
(23, 'shakibi', 29, 5, 29, 'Batman Forever', 1995)
Please rate this movie?:   5
(24, 'shakibi', 45, 5, 45, 'Eat Drink Man Woman', 1994)
Please rate this movie?:   5
(25, 'shakibi', 47, 5, 47, 'Ed Wood', 1994)
Please rate this movie?:   5

-----------THESE ARE YOUR RATINGS---------------
[(16, 'shakibi', 4, 5, 4, 'Get Shorty', 1995), 'rating', 5, (17, 'shakibi', 5, 5, 5, 'Copycat', 1995), 'rating', 5, (18, 'shakibi', 6, 5, 6, 'Shanghai Triad (Yao a yao yao dao waipo qiao)', 1995), 'rating', 4, (19, 'shakibi', 10, 5, 10, 'Richard III', 1996), 'rating', 5, (20, 'shakibi', 18, 5, 18, 'White Balloon, The', 1995), 'rating', 4, (21, 'shakibi', 4, 5, 4, 'Get Shorty', 1995), 'rating', 5, (22, 'shakibi', 13, 5, 13, 'Mighty Aphrodite', 1995), 'rating', 4, (23, 'shakibi', 29, 5, 29, 'Batman Forever', 1995), 'rating', 5, (24, 'shakibi', 45, 5, 45, 'Eat Drink Man Woman', 1994), 'rating', 5, (25, 'shakibi', 47, 5, 47, 'Ed Wood', 1994), 'rating', 5]

-----------OUR RECOMMENDATIONS------------------

Total 5s: 7
Total 4s: 3
Total 4s: 0
Total 4s: 0
Total 4s: 0

We recommend more comedies

Extension Challenges:

❖ Produce a query that incorporates the User's Interests (these were collected at Sign Up) into future recommendations.

❖ Refine the comparison conditions for the ratings and produce further conditions eg using 'ones', 'twos' and 'threes'.

www.ingramcontent.com/pod-product-compliance
Lightning Source LLC
LaVergne TN
LVHW012315070326
832902LV00001BA/15